The *Sales* Dictionary

"Everything comes down to sales."

BY THOMAS S. CALDWELL

Luis

November 1997 – First Printing
July 1998 – Second Printing
March 2001 – Third Printing
March 2002 – Fourth Printing
October 2005 – Fifth Printing
October 2006 – Sixth Printing
August 2007 - Seventh Printing
November 2009 - Eighth Printing

ISBN 0-9683300-0-2
Printed in Canada

With thanks to my dear wife Dorothy for her support, patience and help.

Dedicated to all the people I have worked with over the years.

About the Author

Thomas S. Caldwell's career in the investment industry began in 1965 after he graduated from McGill University with an honours degree in economics. He worked in research and sales in Montreal, New York and Toronto prior to founding Caldwell Securities Ltd. in 1980. As Chairman and Chief Executive Officer of Caldwell Financial Ltd., Mr. Caldwell now oversees brokerage and investment management activities in both Canada and the United States. Caldwell Investment Management Ltd., a subsidiary company, manages the Caldwell family of mutual funds. The overall business has been built by providing quality investment services to clients.

Introduction

I never cease to be amazed that selling, the central economic activity in virtually all societies, is so completely ignored by learning institutions. Perhaps, this is the result of a vision of Willie Loman or the image of someone in a loud suit, with a wide tie, pumping someone's hand up and down to a grinning "Hi ya pal."

Whatever the reason, academia's attempt to deal with selling is usually limited to marketing, which allows those with more fragile egos to avoid coming to grips with fear, self doubt and self-discipline.

To begin, let's define **selling** as *the effective communication of an idea or concept in order*

to influence events and actions. According to this definition, you can see that you have been doing this, to some degree, for your entire life. Whether it was buying a car at a good price, convincing someone to do or not do something, or simply playing on a team, you already have sales experience.

Each word in the definition is weighted. In the following pages, we will examine each and the factors behind them. The definitions or traits noted therein will help to polish and hone skills you already possess and combine them with the organization and discipline needed to achieve success, no matter what your occupation.

You will notice that I have not mentioned a winning personality as a critical factor. It is far down the list of needed ingredients.

Despite the popularized version of the salesperson, the quality most essential for success is honesty. If you do not believe in a product, service, or course of action, then you should not be selling it. You are wasting your time, undermining your reputation and, more seriously, burying your own sense of right and wrong. To be successful, you must honestly believe that your recommendation will bring benefit.

The key factors for success are listed in dictionary form so they are easily accessible. This book is meant to be used in your working day. Blank pages are included at the back for additional definitions which you find particularly helpful. Please forward them to me, for possible inclusion in future editions.

Thomas S. Caldwell
150 King Street West
Suite 1710, P.O. Box 47
Toronto, Ontario
M5H 1J9

A

ACCOMPLISHMENTS – are great. They build self-esteem and confidence. Do not, however, beat yourself up over things you did not do well. They encourage drive and the determination to do better in the future. Each of us has unfinished business or unachieved goals in our past. They can be excellent fuel for other accomplishments. Many people without university degrees have been driven to success by that "lack."

ACTION – You often hear the best ideas from people who obviously never succeeded. The primary reason is that they simply did nothing with their concepts. They never let their ideas stand the test of reality, usually because of fear. Ideas do not have to be great or inspired to bring success, they just have to be intelligently acted upon. Nothing happens until you get into action. Find reasons to act rather than to do nothing. It is easier to act your way into better thinking than to think your way into better acting. If you are doing the "do things," sooner or later your thinking will change and you will succeed.

ADVERSITY – seems to be the key ingredient required for human progress. Only in troubled times are we forced to really look at ourselves and our circumstances. This self-examination can lead to change where we either deal with the adversity or alter the way we look at it. It is often on the latter path where real growth occurs.

ADVERTISING – can add to confusion. People will, in the end, rely on established and trusted relationships. Build on those relationships.

ADVICE – Share what has or has not worked for you in your own experience. Be wary of giving advice in matters you have not experienced. Listen to the advice of others and weigh it on the same basis.

AFFINITY MARKETING – There is usually a thread or tie between an existing client and many other valid prospects. Each client is part of a broader network. He or she may be a franchisee, a member of an organization or fellowship, or simply a golfer who plays regularly with friends. This network is a highway to building your business. Referrals sought from clients will come from this group so be aware of his or her world when asking for the names of prospects.

AGE – "I'm too old to change" – Ebenezer Scrooge. Don't believe it. It wasn't true for him and it is not true for you.

AGREEMENTS – must always be strictly adhered to with no changes or rationalizations.

ALCOHOL – The best way to make a difficult situation appear insurmountable is to pour booze on top of it. Alcohol plays a key role in many suicides. The lack of perspective that results from alcohol use can have less dramatic results. The time, opportunities, self-esteem and relationships put at risk strongly suggest the need to watch for this subtle and patient destroyer.

AMBITION – is a good thing, but try not to let it stand in the way of accomplishment. Ambition relates to self. Accomplishment relates to goals, which often require some self-sacrifice.

ANGER – The cost of this totally destructive emotion cannot be measured in dollars, relationships, pain or self-esteem. There is rarely a constructive purpose achieved or a goal attained by it. Its results are universally negative. Its draining effect can quite literally be felt physically. If you mentally happen upon a "hot spot," you can actually feel the energy drain from your body. Anger is usually sparked by fear and fed with a negative attitude. It takes daily resolve not to allow anger to play a part in your life. As a tool for achieving goals, it must also be discarded.

ANXIETY – Everyone suffers from anxiety to some degree, whether or not it is based on reality. We usually have very little control over the stimuli affecting our emotions, but the net result of unchecked anxiety is highly destructive. It can literally immobilize a person and lead to the very outcome that is most feared.

The best counter to anxiety is to attempt to take your eyes off yourself or your circumstances and try to find a way to be of service or help to someone else. If the anxiety appears to have a business basis, look for a way to help someone in a business sense. For example, you could help a customer or prospect with his or her needs or goals. Anxiety based on other factors can also be handled in the same way. The key is to trust that your needs will be met as you help others to meet theirs.

APPRECIATION – Show it. (See Gratitude.)

APOLOGIES – Never apologize for calling anyone – ever. You are making the effort to provide your professional knowledge, expertise and integrity to assist the prospect to achieve his or her goals. Remember, you are attempting to be of service. If, in the overall business of life, you make a mistake, apologies and amends should be made quickly.

ARROGANCE – Life has a rather brutal way of dealing with arrogance. Try to recognize it in yourself and deal with it. Arrogance is usually fuelled by ignorance. Arrogance is a great way to create enemies.

ASK – "Why?" often. "How?" is also good. There are no foolish questions, unless they are simply attempts to be noticed. The legitimate quest for knowledge and information is normally respected. Try to discern the real underlying factors in the events affecting you or your business.

ASSIGN – tasks. It is the only way to get extra leverage from your time and ideas. Remember, however, that as responsibilities are assigned down the line, they become less important to each subsequent individual.

Follow-up is a key to ensuring that things get done.

ASSUME – positive behaviour and responses from others (clients, prospects, friends, associates and family). Even when you don't receive it, act as if you have. It is amazing how a negative situation can be turned around with positive responses and acts of kindness, consideration and humour.

ATTACK – Always be on the attack – especially when in doubt. Attack. Get going.

ATTITUDE – What actually happens to or around you is not as important as your attitude when it does. There is some good in everything and everyone in this life, yet nothing and no one is perfect. We have, as a consequence, a choice in the way we look at our situation. A negative attitude is necessary for anger, fear and eventually failure. A positive attitude is central to any success and nothing can really be accomplished without it. Your attitude is the single most important factor in determining the outcome of any situation or endeavour. It is more important than skills, training, background or anything else.

ATTRACTION – rather than self-promotion is the best way to build and establish relationships. Be enthusiastic and upbeat about your work, your company and your associates. You will be amazed how people are then drawn to you.

AVAILABILITY – is a key ingredient for sales. Being involved in life will put you in contact with others. People are interested in what others do and like to deal with those they know and respect. The more activities you are involved in, the greater will be your availability to others. Casually talking about your product or profession often gives you the opportunity for a "soft sales" conversation.

B

BEHAVIOUR – Always conduct yourself so that it would not matter if your actions were shown on television. Strive to be consistent with what you say. What you do says more about you than what you say. Be proud of yourself, not prideful.

BELIEVE – in yourself, your product, your skills, your company and your integrity. Without the assurance which comes from this, your results will be mediocre at best. Believe that God wants you to do your best to be of service to others, in a business sense and in other ways. This conviction will see you through many sparse and dark periods.

BENEFIT – The benefit of a product, service or course of action should be compelling. It has to be something the prospect already wants, for example, financial security etc. When an action or decision is recommended, the prospect will often pause. He or she will reflect on reasons why not to act. Your task is to reinforce the need for action by emphasizing the benefit(s) of your product.

For you to know what the prospect wants, you must find out prior to attempting to close what his or her goals and objectives are. Probing questions can increase the confidence of prospects so that they will give you their real objectives. The key to a compelling benefit is finding out what the prospect really wants, and then addressing it. This will help you replace superficial negatives.

BEST – Do your best each day. Don't be half-baked in your approach to business or anything else. The results from doing your best (or even trying to) are totally predictable.

THE BIBLE – A source of strength and guidance that specifically addresses every area of human need. Someone once described it as "The Manufacturer's Handbook" and, as such, it has all the instructions we require. Even for agnostics, it can be considered the accumulation of wisdom over the ages. This valuable resource should not be ignored, in either good or bad times.

BLAME – Blaming others is almost a certain guarantee that you will not learn or progress from setbacks. Ask yourself what your part in the problem was and how you can change or benefit from it.

Get out of the blame business – most participants in a deal know who is responsible.

BOND – We usually bond with people when we have common experiences or do things with them. Get together in some format with clients and prospects to develop relationships.

BOOKS – Nonfiction is vastly more beneficial than fiction. You want to know what real people did in real circumstances, and how it worked out. This can provide both encouragement and a basis for identification. History is a great teacher. It is a pity that we so thoroughly ignore it or mutilate it.

BREAK-UP – It seems that only after the break-up of a business or personal relationship do we see those things we could have, or should have, done. Try to consider positive actions before a break-up. Look ahead and see the other person's point of view. (See Gratitude.)

BUILD-UP – Advertising, mailings and media exposure are like artillery. They soften up the objective and let everyone know what is to follow. Remember, however, that nothing really happens until individuals move forward to achieve a goal. Successful selling usually requires a build-up or introductory phase with material and information to introduce your company, your services and yourself. Move as quickly as you can from this phase to making contact with the prospect – preferably personal contact.

C

CALL – Nothing happens until you make a call.

CALL BACK – Do not assume the reason for someone's call. Call them back. You will often be surprised. Returning calls is a form of advertising. It establishes the courtesy, efficiency and service attitude of your organization and yourself. No one is so important they cannot return all calls by the end of the business day.

CAN'T – is a word that should rarely be used. Be honest with yourself and use the real word – won't.

CAREER – Remember that character is more important than career. Just as God is more concerned with the inner person, so should we be. If you build your character, your career will follow.

CAREERIST – Someone who sees a job as simply a means to getting a better one. Consistently doing the best you can is probably one of the better methods of advancement. This means putting a high value on one's job, customers and fellow workers. Going for short-term glory or opportunity in order to move on breeds resentment from all quarters. Careerists are seen as "time wasters" as soon as their real motivation is understood.

CASUAL – Do not be casual in your dress, your attitudes, your work or in the service or products you wish to provide. Customers have a right to expect your best at all times.

CHARACTER – is defined and built in adversity, not success.

CHECKS AND BALANCES – should exist for all key tasks. People forget or make mistakes. At a minimum, keep a record of critical functions: who is responsible and how and when the work is to be verified.

CHOICE – Each day, you choose what you are going to do or what you will attempt to accomplish. If you do not make this conscious choice, then it is usually made for you by circumstances or events. The more external forces make these choices for you, through your own default, then the greater the possibility that you will eventually lose the option of choice in your endeavours altogether. You can choose what you are going to think and worry about. You can also choose to have a good time.

CIRCUMSTANCES -Your current situation or circumstance is not necessarily an indicator of your future possibilities. Your situation is a reflection of what has gone on before, but attitudes, focus, change, skills, faith and determination are what will decide the future.

CLEAN – yourself up. Recognize and come to grips with character defects such as low self-image, fear and the craving for acceptance from others that continually sabotage ability. Externals such as appearance are also important.

CLIENT FIRST – Such an attitude will be recognized and rewarded. People know when you are "for" them and when you're not. Any true success will be based on the former approach, because money and, for that matter, happiness are by-products of service to others. Put your clients first and yourself third (just in case you are getting too close being second).

CLOSAPHOBIA – is the fear of "closing." The number of salespeople that are prepared to accept a slew of "maybes" or "laters" rather than seek a clear decision is astounding. Truly confident professionals want the facts so that they can be of service to the prospect or to someone else. The "nos" won't kill you, the "maybes" will.

It is said that "the truth shall make you free." Seeking it with caring and courage will save you time and build your own sense of self-worth.

CLOSE THE LOOP – Ninety-percent is great in school, but it can be a disaster in business. Because all of our actions are inter-related, items left undone or not communicated can cost both time and money. When working on any project (or giving instructions) make sure everyone involved is clearly informed. As a team, organizations can only excel by "closing the loop."

CLOSING – is the logical conclusion when a qualified prospect has been presented with a clear presentation outlining how and why this product or service will address his or her needs, goals or ambitions. The simple reasons for action have been made, the benefits are clear and the cost is worthwhile and achievable.

Often, the qualified prospect may hesitate – decisions carry the possibility of making mistakes. Your task is not only to reassure with the facts, but occasionally to stimulate the individual into making the correct decision. This is not a pressure technique, but an attempt to show the consequences or disadvantages of an incorrect decision or of no decision. This can take the form of a "disturbing" question. Make it easy for the qualified prospect to act. Do not be confrontational – be on the same team with him or her to achieve the goal.

In closing, make a directive to action, not simply a suggestion. People want solutions to their problems, not more data to make their own choices.

Not closing is often more of a fear thing than a lack of technique. There is a time in a presentation to move to action – you will know it at the time. (See Peak.)

None of these steps are to be construed as pressure tactics. You are simply presenting a logical choice so that a correct decision is made from clear information.

COERCION – is the crudest and lowest form of influence. Avoid it as much as possible.

COLD CALL – Be clear and courteous to your prospect's secretary and do not mislead or be untruthful about your purpose. This does not mean, however, that you elaborate fully about your call to anyone other than your prospect.

Very often the screening secretary can be helpful, if given the opportunity. Do not leave a message for the prospect to return your call. Leave your name and offer to call back at a more convenient time.

Never start a prospect conversation with "How are you today?" It brands you as a hypocrite, pretending to be a friend and not really caring to hear a true response. To most people, this is a very irritating greeting from a pure stranger.

Greet your prospect, using his or her name, and then quickly introduce yourself, your firm and state the purpose of your call. Remember, in most cases, you have been preceded by a letter, brochure, marked-up news clipping or research report (which has probably been lost), so this is not purely a cold call.

In this conversation, be clear, positive and enthusiastic. Have a copy of the key points of your call in front of you. If you are simply making a bland offering, the results are predictable. If you honestly believe in your product, act accordingly. It may take several more calls and ideas, as well as a face-to-face meeting, but the probability of success is with you.

This first call is really a probing exercise to obtain information and to find a reason for future contact. Be prepared to allow the prospect to talk. Questions followed by silence will enable you to determine his or her needs.

COMMISSIONS – are an index of your service to others. They measure the effectiveness of your actions as they relate to helping others with their needs.

COMMITMENT – to your own success is necessary. You must root out those things (external and internal) which stand in the way of true progress. Commitment will keep you going when others fall by the wayside.

COMMITMENTS – They must always be kept. Your word and your reputation must be as solid as a rock.

COMMON SENSE – can save a lot of wasted time and effort. Why are you doing a thing? What is the goal? Is the deal reasonable? Can it be explained easily? Would you buy this product? Basic, God-given intelligence will provide many answers and clear direction. Be careful when the deal is too complicated.

COMMUNICATE – Express your ideas and/or information in a manner your prospect can understand and relate to. Professionals and salespeople often use the jargon of their particular trades which the prospects simply do not understand.

Communicating clearly and effectively is also critical to the internal functioning of your organization. Teams cannot achieve goals without members connecting with one another. Communicating your plans, goals and problems to your manager is of major importance. All companies are in the communications business.

COMPROMISE – If you do not stick to what you know is right, you kill your self-esteem, the respect of others and the momentum required for victory. Change your stance only if you are not right.

CONCENTRATE – Focus on your goal, and the steps to achieving it, on an hourly, daily, weekly or yearly basis. Be ruthless with distractions, no matter how alluring. Concentrate on the means of success, not the symptoms of failure.

CONFIDENCE – comes from believing that you are doing the right thing for your customer or prospect. If you were certain that a great disaster would befall your neighbours unless you warned them, you would be in touch with all of them immediately. The same is true of a great benefit. The variable between these circumstances and your business is the amount of benefit and your belief in it. Confidence is central to both sales and leadership. If you do not have it, no one else will.

CONFUSION – You are often the most confused at turning points. Try to see what is really important within the information you have. Where will the different decisions lead? Common sense and what is right are great guides. (See Decisions.)

CONNECT – with others, even if it is only to say "Good Morning." Use the other person's name if possible. You can improve someone else's day simply by greeting him or her – make a point of doing it. This, in turn, will establish you as a caring and interested person.

CONSIDERATION – The Golden Rule – treat others as you wish to be treated. The backlash from inconsiderate behaviour is predictable and can have a negative impact on your reputation, relationships and business. Seeing people as important is the key to being of service to others. This is what business, and life for that matter, is all about.

CONSISTENCY – Strive to be consistent in your actions and statements. A reputation for dependability and trustworthiness comes from consistent behaviour.

CONTROL – the agenda. You have meetings for a purpose. Stay focused on your goal and work toward it in a straight line, as much as that is possible. Do not let the prospect drag you all over the verbal countryside with side issues. Yes, address concerns, but stay on target.

CORRESPONDENCE – Keep it simple and short.

COURAGE – and honesty go together. This includes the willingness to honestly look at ourselves. Have the courage to change, to admit mistakes and to praise others. We are not talking about the courage to charge up a hill, but to confront our own fears and insecurities. This is tougher stuff than mere physical daring.

CRITICISM – People find it is much easier to be against things than to be part of a group or process to make things better. Looking for what is right or good and trying to build on the existing positives is an exercise in maturity. Criticize actions or events, not the people themselves. First determine if the issue is important enough. Leave people room to save face.

CROSS PURPOSES – Avoid meetings with more than one agenda – one where you are seeking a certain goal and the prospect has a totally different objective. When two people are trying to sell each other their product or service, neither is listening to the other person's presentation. Instead, they are looking for opportunities to make their own points. Two separate meetings at different times would ensure that the agenda for each is clear.

CUMULATIVE – Very little that anyone ever does is wasted. Everything can be used in some manner for some good purpose. You may often feel that your efforts are simply going out into the void and nothing will ever come of them. Doing the right thing consistently brings results, sometimes years later.

CUSTOMER (OR CLIENT) – The person, persons or organizations that collectively pay all our bills and those of our companies in exchange for receiving services or products that meet their needs. The value of customers is total and we must continually remind ourselves of their worth, particularly when they behave in a difficult or demanding manner or when we ourselves are stressed out or tired. We are not called upon to be subservient to our customers, but we should at least attempt to see things from their perspective and respond positively. Our customers can also be our most effective salespeople. (See Gratitude.)

D

DECISIONS – If you have to make an important decision try these three steps: First, pray. You want to be in line with God's will and seek His direction. If you do not have a faith – pray anyway. At a minimum, you will hear yourself more honestly articulate the alternatives.

Second, talk to someone else. Most of us are rationalists and should seek an outside opinion in order to make sure our wants or emotions are not colouring our view of things. Third, wait until your choice "feels comfortable." Sometimes, deep down, as a result of a number of small factors, we know the answer. This is where common sense comes from. These steps help to quell emotions before making decisions.

Never make a decision in front of anyone else. Getting back to someone may cause you to miss the occasional deal, but using these steps will dramatically improve the quality and results of your decision-making.

Keep in mind, if you avoid making decisions, they are usually made for you and often not the way you would have wished. No decision is still a decision.

DEFEAT – only exists when it is accepted. The seeds of victory are within every setback. Get the positive(s) out of every negative, i.e., learn.

DEGREES – Don't take them too seriously, particularly if you have one or more. Degrees can be helpful in government or teaching, but in the real world, determination, common sense and a clear sense of right and wrong are the requirements for success.

DEPENDABILITY – Business is based on trust. "On time, on budget and as promised" are the norm for successful careers and enterprises. When given an instruction, carry it out fully and report back. Dependability and greater responsibility go together.

DIFFICULTIES – plague everyone from time to time. Deal with them the best way you can. Breaking them down into bite-sized pieces can sometimes help. Trying to avoid difficulties very often leads to bigger problems.

DISCIPLINE – is internal. It is how we rule ourselves, our emotions, our fatigue, our hunger etc. Doing what should be done is the result of internal discipline not the discipline itself. Self-discipline and self-esteem are connected.

DISCOURAGEMENT – "This too shall pass." A few steps which can help:

(a) View your present situation as temporary.
(b) Do your best, one day at a time.
(c) Ask for help – pray.
(d Have faith. Believe that things will get better.
(e) Ask yourself: What is the next positive thing I can do?

DREAM – If you are going to dream, dream big – then get on with it.

DRESS – conservatively. You can be assured that your prospect will be looking at your suit, hair, shoes etc., grasping for some tip-off as to your personality, maturity and success. Do not overdo the image thing, but don't sabotage yourself prior to letting your ideas and ability establish your calibre. Dress often indicates what you think of yourself and your customers.

DRUGS – If you use chemicals to live in the real world, you have a problem. It doesn't matter if you pop them, sip them, shoot them or smoke them. (See Alcohol.)

E

EFFORT – Always give things 100 percent of your time, effort and energy or don't bother. A ninety percent effort leaves ten percent to cause chaos and resentment in an inter-dependent environment or team effort such as business. Do not rationalize poor effort on the basis of a change in priorities.

EMOTIONS – cost money. Instincts make it. (See Fitness.)

EMPLOYER – Know whom you represent. Find out everything you can about your company, its products, its culture, its connections and your associates and their skills.

Always build-up your firm and the people in it. This will, in turn, build you. If you are negative about your company and associates, the first question a client will ask himself is "why is he there?" Praising the skills and abilities of your fellow employees enhances you as part of a winning team.

ENCOURAGE – others. This is the best way to get the full potential from your fellow workers and friends. Be part of the success of others.

ENERGY – We occasionally lack the strength to keep going. Get into action – do something even slightly productive and you will be surprised how your energy comes back. To succeed in sales one must develop and maintain a high energy level. (See Procrastination and Fitness.)

ENTERTAINMENT – can be important to sales, but not as critical as many think. The important factor is to provide a good product on a competitive basis, and to inform people that you and your organization consistently do so. Many successful people do very little entertaining. The amount depends on what you are comfortable with and what works for you, your product and your company.

ENTHUSIASM – In the final analysis, it is your enthusiasm for a product or course of action that sells. It is infectious. If you do not have enthusiasm between the opportunity and success, you have a brick wall.

ESCAPISM – comes in many guises. It can take the form of substitute accomplishments, good works, family and social commitments or a focus on micro issues. Try to recognize it and get back on track.

EXERCISE – Regular physical exercise is essential to long-term business success. Get into a routine and you will find it helps with tension, fear, anxiety and low self-esteem. Your brain will also work better.

EXPAND – your world. Be part of a world larger than your business interests or job. Be of service in the wider spectrum of life. Numerous friends and contacts are a by-product of helping others.

EXPERIENCE – is invaluable if we benefit from it and use it, either to help ourselves or others. Very little in our lives is ever wasted and even the difficult things we suffer through can be used in some way. A philosopher once said, "those things that don't kill us, make us stronger."

EXPERTS – Beware of them and don't be intimidated by them. Specific knowledge is often necessary, but it should not be confused with good common sense or wisdom. Experts sometimes get confused in this matter, as well as do those who are mesmerized by them.

EXTEND – yourself, your reach and your abilities. Try to do that extra push-up, jog that extra hundred yards, or attempt to do slightly more than you have been able to accomplish in the past. You don't need to climb mountains every week-end, but push slightly beyond your comfort or safe zone. By doing so, it will be expanded and so will your confidence and sense of self-worth.

EXTRA – Always try to go that extra mile. This kind of service is what ongoing customer loyalty is built on. Personally pick up that cheque or documentation, drop in to see customers, especially when a sale is not imminent, send articles of interest etc. It's similar to an additional two miles to the ice cream parlour that gives that extra scoop or the hardware store that provides that extra service. Giving extra can overcome most competitive disadvantages.

To some extent, this means putting your faith in people to respond. Occasionally you will be let down, but in the long run your overall effort will be rewarded. This principle also holds true within your office or company.

EXTREMES – Avoid extremes in thought, word and deed. They point to immaturity and an unwillingness to be open or to learn. They also scare people.

F

FAILURE – To be a failure requires making many wrong decisions over a prolonged period, and then giving up. Failure is not a one decision thing. What most people call failures are really just setbacks. The seeds of victory are within every setback. (See Setbacks.) Failure is not trying and the results are quite predictable.

FAITH – has been described as the "substance of things hoped for." Anyone who has played a sport or been in a game has experienced this especially when the score is against you. It is suddenly knowing you can win. It's a confidence that speaks clearly, revitalizes and usually leads to victory. Work on building faith in your God, yourself and your product. It is a clear path to victory and not much happens without it.

Faith is your best weapon against despair in times of adversity. It should be in place before the trouble begins, just as defenses should be built up before an attack. There is little time to do so during the event.

FAMILY – Their needs and goals should align with those of your business. Do not continually sacrifice one for the other. You and your spouse should agree on career commitments. By the same token, many use family considerations as an excuse for half-hearted business efforts. Generally speaking, your family should benefit from the lifestyle and choices provided through financial success. They should not be continually sacrificed to attain it. Family goals should be part of your career goals and vice versa.

FATIGUE – Emotional or physical fatigue expands the tasks facing us and diminishes our ability and resolve to deal with them. Very often however, it is a symptom rather than a cause. It is frequently the result of procrastination. If you are not doing those things you know you must, your energy evaporates. The counter to fatigue can be as simple as cleaning up your desk, putting your records in order, or making a few calls. Action, however small, is often the antidote for fatigue. Fatigue can cause us to see a customer as an irritation or interruption rather than the purpose of business. Watch for this, it is a symptom of burn-out.

FEAR – can immobilize anyone. Separate real fear from irrational fear. In order to see if there is anything that you can do about it, write down your concerns and attempt to find the root cause. This usually provides an answer – often simple, like fatigue, or not doing what you should be doing, or not getting your own way, or lack of faith etc. In these cases, fear is a warning bell, reminding you of the basics. Irrational fear, over and above these cases, usually needs to be fed by low self-esteem, lack of confidence, or a negative attitude. Although destructive in result, this type of fear is a phantom, in that it has no basis in external threat.

Another thing to do when confronted with real fear is to shrink your time frame to one day or one hour etc. Anyone can handle virtually anything in small amounts. It is only when we extrapolate into the future, or look back, that we have difficulty. (See Anxiety.)

Many people are so afraid of failure that they do not really try. They assume that if a real effort is not made, then they have not really failed. Success is another great fear because of new responsibilities and challenges. Both of these fears are based on low self-image or self-esteem.

Many of us must wrestle with fear on a regular basis. Unchecked, it can totally immobilize an individual. Recognize it and deal with it. The counter to fear is faith.

F.I.D.O. – "Forget it, drive on." Do not hang on to old hurts and grudges. Keep moving forward and try to leave those burdens behind you.

FINANCIAL PROBLEMS – rarely exist. Financial symptoms are the norm. What we often see as problems are in reality, symptoms of the real problem(s). With individuals, the real or underlying problem can be alcohol, drugs, attitudes, focus etc. With companies it can be product, services, courtesy, location, lack of customer appreciation etc. Find and deal with the "real" problem and financial symptoms will evaporate.

FIRST CLASS – Think and act first class in all things and at all times.

FIRST IMPRESSIONS – How many times can you make a first impression on a person? A bad first impression is very difficult to overcome. It is far easier to arrive appropriately dressed and well spoken, than have to engage in damage control later.

FIRST NAMES – Many salespeople try to use a prospect's first name immediately, in order to build an instantaneous personal connection. Usually it doesn't work and is generally seen as simply a technique. Often, this lack of respect and jumping into familiarity raises suspicions as to the salesperson's overall integrity and professionalism.

FITNESS – We are mental, physical and spiritual beings who require exercise, rest and nutrition in each of these areas. Look at your attitudes, emotions and habits as well as the operating basis for your life. In order to achieve excellence throughout a career and lifetime, long-term fitness across this threefold spectrum is mandatory. Consider yourself in a business marathon. Deal with those things which you know are harmful. (See Emotions, Exercise and Spiritual.)

FOCUS – externally. Try to be of service to others, and help them with their needs and concerns. Financial rewards and job satisfaction come as a by-product of addressing the needs of others. If you focus on small goals, you will probably achieve them. If you focus on large goals, and work toward them daily, you will probably achieve them, in addition to all your smaller goals.

Try to avoid a self-centered or personal focus, such as bills, personal concerns, problems, needs and ambitions etc.

Watch for distractions and substitutes for action – they are time wasters. Stay on target and know what you are trying to do and achieve. Concentrate your ideas into your products and actions.

FOLLOW-UP – Post sales follow-up is central to further sales and referrals. Checking back to see if the goods are satisfactory, meet the prospect's needs, or to reinforce an earlier sales commitment shows you care and that you are not simply mercenary. People respond very favourably to this continuing interest in their welfare, and quite negatively when you do not show it. It's almost like thanking a person for a date or dinner the next day. Follow-up has the added bonus of being an opportune time to widen your client base through referrals.

The best time to make a follow-up call on a mailing is before the mailing arrives. This flags it to your prospect and gives you a reason for a second call after its arrival. Follow-up calls before the fact can help to ensure that your material is not thrown out. A follow-up call on a mailing a week or so later is a waste of time. The prospect won't remember receiving your material.

FORGOT – "Sorry, I forgot" is not an acceptable excuse in any organization. You are responsible for remembering. Write everything down if you have to.

FRIENDS – To make and keep friends requires a little consideration. To make and keep enemies requires none. People like to deal with their friends – give contacts good reason to consider you one.

FUN – Have fun.

G

GIVING UP – "Never give in! Never give in! Never, never, never, never – in nothing great or small, large or petty – never give in except to convictions of honour and good sense." – Winston Churchill's speech at Harrow School after the Second World War.

GLORY – In most projects, endeavours or companies, there is glory enough for all. Don't seek it – share it. Build up others. Those who try to grab glory for themselves, rarely get any.

GOALS – Establish achievable goals and write them down. Break goals up into bite-sized pieces by amount or time frame such as, daily or weekly objectives. This will help you to work "in the now" versus having some lofty, distant objective. When you achieve your goal(s) on a consistent basis, then escalate it or them in order to move to the next plateau. Be very careful about completely changing your goals and certainly don't do it very often. It is a tip-off to giving up.

GOD – wants good things to happen to you. As you develop a faith in Him you will not only have a reference point for all your dealings, but you will be able to endure and accomplish far beyond that which you can suffer and achieve in your own strength. Also keep in mind that any god but the real God will kill you. Don't make your business your God.

GOSSIP – talks about a person instead of to them. Gossip is never based on caring for others.

GRACE – The highest form of compassion is grace. It is kindness and forgiveness when they are not deserved. Most of us need some grace in our lives. Try to provide some for others.

GRATITUDE – If you are not grateful for what you have, you are probably going to lose it. This holds for a job, a customer, an employee, a friend, a relationship, or almost anything else. Practicing gratitude is a great way to overcome depression and negativity. It is a foundation for happiness. Show your appreciation to others.

GROWTH – is often painful and sometimes frightening. More often than not, we are forced to grow by things that happen or things that we do or don't do. Without growth, nothing really changes. We simply move in and out of the same circumstances or situations. Internal and external progress go together.

GUIDANCE – Very often qualified prospects look to the salesperson to recommend a course of action or provide guidance. He or she may see the benefit in a course of action but not know how much or when to make a purchase. This is where personal character comes into play. Your honesty, courage and caring attitude are central to the qualified prospect making the right decision. Time will tell whether those characteristics were properly in play.

H

HANGING IN – is sometimes winning. Continuing your efforts during those difficult or sparse periods often brings victory.

HELP – The only people who can be helped are those who want to be helped. This is true in personal as well as business matters.

HERE TO THERE – When you don't know how to get from here to there, wait for inspiration. For those who can pray, seek God's guidance. Occasionally talking to others can help, even if you don't take their advice.

HIDE – Don't hide from issues, decisions or new information. Be open and ready to address what needs to be done. People often hide using pride in life or business. (See Pride.)

HIGH GROUND – In any battle or contest, it has always been important to fight on your own terms and on terrain favourable to you.

Typically, this means taking and holding the high ground, from which you can look down upon your enemies and force them to attack in a disadvantageous up-hill battle. The discipline was not to get lured or angered into fighting on the enemy's terms or terrain.

The high ground in sales is your effort to provide quality, caring and professional service to customers. Keep this in the forefront of all of your presentations.

Do not get lured into a numbers game, name calling or competitor bashing. This will demean your standards and cloud your message. It can lure you from the heights to fight in a swamp, wherein you lose the advantage.

If you are genuinely trying to do the right thing for prospects and customers, it will shine through, even if you make mistakes in your presentation. Take and hold on to the high ground.

HOLIDAYS – If you don't take holidays you will get sick. Whether they are short or long, take breaks from your work for the sake of yourself, your family, your fellow employees and your customers.

HONESTY – means: "I told the prospect or client the details of a transaction." Rigorous honesty means: "I made sure he or she understood all the key points." Aim for the latter. If you are known to be honest, you will more than make up for your failings. If you are seen as dishonest, it won't matter what your assets are.

HOPE – is a key ingredient for life. Without hope we are ready to die. Fear often undercuts action or real effort, which in time robs us of self-esteem and hope. This usually results in our simply giving up. Work at having hope for the future, for your ideas and your possibilities. Look at the positive factors in the present, and extend them down the road into the future.

HUMILITY – One thing is certain about humility – if you don't seek it, it will be provided. Be open to learn and grow.

HUMOUR – Try to keep a sense of humour about yourself and your circumstances. It will help with perspective. Sometimes it takes a real effort, but not taking things too seriously can be an emotional escape valve. Be careful when you lose your ability to laugh.

Humour in small doses (and only if you are funny) can be used in sales presentations as a check to see if the prospect is "tuned in." How quickly he or she laughs can tell you how well you are connecting.

Think as to the subject of your humour. Avoid put-down, racist, sexist or off-colour jokes.

I

IDEAS – People buy into an idea rather than an object. The idea and its allure are what draw people in. It must be valid for the product to be valid. For example, are they buying a car for safety, prestige or a self statement? The idea is the essence of the reason for action or the underlying benefit that the prospect sees.

IMPORTANT – There is not a great deal in life that is truly important, but what is important is usually very important. Determine what is important, then address it and leave the rest.

IMPRESS – Trying to impress others usually has the exact opposite effect. Efforts to impress someone can hamper our ability to listen, compel us to interrupt in order to be noticed, and generally cut us off from others. There are many other examples of this. The desire to impress is a symptom of insecurity or low self-esteem and works against us. Relax. Be yourself. That's more than enough.

INDECISION – Be very careful about changing your decisions. Usually your first decision is right. Unless you acquire totally new information, changes are often based on fear.

INFORMATION – is power. Listen and communicate effectively. Share information with those on your team. Ask for their input to avoid surprises.

INJUSTICE – The world is filled with injustices. The conversations of many (possibly most) people are based on the petty injustices they have suffered at the hands of bosses, spouses, bank tellers, store clerks etc. This is not only boring and negative, but also is a major energy drain. The only way to get out of this rut and deal with injustice is through forgiveness. Although often you may feel it is undeserved.

INNOVATIVE – Always be looking for a better way of doing things. Ask: "Why?"

INSTINCTS – Trust them. They are often experiences nudging us. A "gut feeling" tends to become more reliable with age. (See Emotions.)

INTERVIEW – The real job or prospect interview begins before the face-to-face meeting. Did you call back when you said you would? Were you there on time (i.e., five minutes early)? Did you send any additional material to the interviewer as promised? Did you show gratitude for having the meeting? The list goes on. You are judged before you even show up as well as afterwards.

INVEST – in yourself, your business and your career. Take courses, go to seminars, spend time to build your product knowledge, read, advertise – in short, do everything possible to be the best in your industry and be recognized as such. Your investment in yourself also includes your appearance, business attire and support items such as a reasonable car that is kept clean. A cellular telephone can assist you in being of service while you are out of the office. This latter item is now a necessity, not a luxury. Your customers expect it.

INVENTORY – From time to time take an inventory of yourself – write down what you consider to be your assets and your liabilities. Look at why you do things. Examine selfishness, greed, self-will, habits, situations, relationships etc. Don't beat yourself up (there are always others available to do that), but try to be objective in order to spot areas for improvement. We are all trying to get better at what we do and improve who we are.

J

JOBS – There are more good jobs than there are good people to fill them. Attitude, skills and experience must be packaged and presented or "sold" to the real decision makers in order to land the position you should have.

JOURNEY – We are all on a journey without the certainty of arriving. Enjoy the journey as best you can, and as you look back you will find that even the dead-ends were not wastes of time. Pressing on and doing your best, one day at a time, will lead you to a place of victory, even if it was not the original goal. We often set our sights too low and end up far beyond our imaginings.

JUDGEMENT – Good judgement comes from experience, and experience comes from bad judgement.

K

KINDNESS – is one of the best investments you can make. It bears great dividends, not only for yourself but for others as well. It is infectious. Always take the time to be kind to others.

KNOW – your product, what it does, what needs it answers and why it is the best. Know your competition's products as well, so you can guide your prospect to the right decision. Know the underlying need that your physical product or service answers. This is the key to a successful sales presentation.

L

LAUGH – at yourself and your circumstances as often as you can. It shows you are not taking either too seriously and it is a sign of good mental health.

LEADERSHIP – The "follow me" kind of leadership, or the power of example, speaks far louder to those you wish to motivate than any lecture. Integrity in action will draw people to your way of doing things. As you achieve success, people watching (other achievers) will seek to emulate your actions. The best way to instruct is to share what you have done and what you are doing. Each of us is a leader through our power of example. Leadership is not a reward, but a responsibility. Good leadership brings out the best in others.

LEARNING – One of the best ways to learn a lesson is to share it with others. We learn by listening, seeing or experiencing. Sadly, most of us have to experience a thing first hand in order to learn. Experience is generally the most painful way to learn, but certainly the most effective – if we survive.

LIFE – is a "come as you are" affair. Get on with it and try to improve and deal with things as you go.

LISTEN – Don't shut off inputs by talking too much. Get the facts straight and forget about trying to impress. Listen to both what is said and what is not. Show that you are interested. Listen with your whole body.

Remember, what people say and what they are telling you are often quite different. Do not let a case of nerves, or an ironclad presentation, interfere with getting the facts needed to be of service. Occasionally a probing question will clarify a prospect's true needs and fears.

LONG-TERM – All of our actions are short-term. The net cumulative total of our daily efforts result in achieving long-term goals. Plan for the future, but act upon it now.

LOSER – Being a loser is a personal decision that only you can make.

LOYALTY – is not a dated concept. If you expect loyalty then you must give it to employees and customers alike. Organizations which demand it up the line, yet never give it down the line, are ongoing disasters in terms of morale. Be loyal, fair, supportive and considerate to your customers and associates (that does not mean being a marshmallow) and they will more than reciprocate in kind. Loyalty has a cost, but it also pays substantial dividends – in terms of the efficiencies that come from long-term employees and customers.

M

MAILINGS – Letters or résumés mean very little unless they are followed up with a call and/or meeting. Too many people mail out material expecting the receiver to jump on the telephone and respond. Things simply don't work that way. Be specific as to the purpose of your letter, for example, the product you are offering or the job or assignment you are seeking and why. Advance notice to your prospect is a good way to ensure that your material will be read. He or she knows you will also be following up with another call.

MANAGING – One of the dangers in managing is over-managing. Give clear instructions, mandates, information etc., then get out of the way. Let people do their work and use their brains. Managers can fool themselves into thinking they're being productive, when in fact, they are slowing things down or interfering.

MEETINGS – Prospect and client meetings are essential for success. The more direct, face-to-face contacts you have with your customers – the better. Organizational or internal corporate meetings are not always necessary. Indeed, they often become impediments to success when they become ends in themselves, rather than the means to goals. When organizing a meeting, ask yourself if it is really necessary, and what you want to achieve. Have a clear agenda and a fixed start and finish time. Keep it brief and to the point.

MESSES – Most messes are messages. They are telling you something.

MINOR DETAILS – Often, individuals or management groups get caught up in micro issues. This occurs when they have lost their overall strategic view and/or confidence in themselves. Ask: How important is it?

Some years ago, an airplane crashed in the Everglades because the flight crew focused on a minor instrument problem, rather than the direction of the aircraft.

MISTAKES – Everyone makes mistakes. Don't be afraid to admit them. It will show strength and confidence. Attempt to learn from them, and try not to beat yourself up over them. Keep your perspective and your sense of humour, and then move on, a little wiser for the experience.

MONEY – should be a servant to do good or to help others. It should not be used to intimidate people or to show off. Money is often an index of service to others.

MOTIVATION – is that desire for, and commitment to, your own success. It is important for both you and your prospects. In action, it shows up as the determination to go the distance, do what is necessary, stay committed, get better, plug energy leaks, get rid of bad habits and see yourself as successful.

MOTIVES – Watch for good motives covering bad motives, particularly when you are offering criticism or advice.

N

NEEDS – If you focus on your clients' or prospects' needs, your own will be met.

NEGATIVES – Focusing on negatives can destroy both companies and individuals. Television is a great source of negatives.

You can't accomplish very much by seeking, concentrating on, or stressing negatives. They are time wasters and energy drains.

NEW BUSINESS – is the life blood of any enterprise. If you are not going forward, you are going backward. All salespeoples' incomes are literally dependent on the new business brought in each month. Simply servicing existing accounts is a "running down" affair. Clients leave, die or go out of business. Therefore you must continually seek new clients throughout your career.

NO – is acceptable only when you say it. Question why the prospect is saying no. Does he or she understand? Is the timing right? Sometimes, probing can turn the situation around to "yes."

A more interesting "no" is your use of it. There will be many times when you, as a salesperson, should turn down business. For example, ethical reasons, difficult or abusive customers, or orders you know will not work out for the participants. It is hard to turn down business, but it will build your reputation, your self esteem and give you more time for problem-free dealings.

NOW – Do it now. Do not let the tasks necessary for success pileup. Get on with them, and avoid procrastination. Put in extra hours to get caught up if necessary, then move forward.

O

OBSTACLES – usually appear bigger before they are attacked. Deal with them step-by-step.

ONCE – Touch papers on your desk only once. Do not examine them and stack them up for later action. Deal with them immediately. Forward them and attach notes or throw them out. Keep the deck clear for action. Treat mini-items coming across your desk like hot potatoes – spend no time handling them – get rid of them with a quick decision.

ONE DAY AT A TIME – Fight your battles in day-tight compartments. Don't look too far back or too far forward. Do your best each day. Review each day to see if what you have done has moved you closer to your goals. If not, try to do better the next day. Occasionally, when you are under stress, you may be able to function only one hour or ten minutes at a time. Just keep inching forward without the baggage from the past or the anxieties of the future.

ORGANIZATION – Being organized is central to building relationships. People who fail to follow through on their commitments are often seen as dishonest, unreliable or uncaring. However, in many cases, they are simply disorganized. Write all commitments and the requests or wishes of your customers (or friends) down in a book. You will be amazed at people's surprise and appreciation when you deliver the goods, even when the request or commitment was simply a passing comment.

Being organized will build your reputation as being reliable and considerate. It is also the key to sales success.

OTHERS – Do not diminish others or hurt their self esteem. This will only reap negatives. If you have done this, clean it up quickly with an apology. Putting others first will inspire those around you, and establish your leadership.

OUT – You have to get out to get the clients in.

OUTFLOW – If your financial outflow is greater than your income, your upkeep will be your downfall. Live within your means and build. Stretching yourself can be good, but catch up on a regular basis.

P

PACKAGING – Consider how you package yourself and your product. Dress, manner of speech and attitude are all part of your packaging. The real underlying need your product meets is also a packaging consideration.

PAST – Many appraisals, decisions and actions are based on history, rather than on the future. Although the past is an important tool, include "what can be" in your thought processes. Future possibilities are the keys to progress. Have a vision.

Don't dwell on the past. What has happened has happened. Don't drag past hurts around with you like Jacob Marley's chains. Move forward from today, unburdened.

PATIENCE – There is a time to "let go and let God." This is very hard for most people. After you have done your very best, and can realistically see no further action that can be taken, back off and let the weight of your efforts sink in. Often we can defeat our own purpose by not letting the prospect thoughtfully consider the product or course of action.

PEAK – that moment in any presentation when the prospect gives the go ahead, be it silence or an affirmative statement, or sometimes a question. Anyone who has been in a selling situation, and is aware of the other person, can recognize the time when closing the sale should be attempted. At this moment the salesperson must separate himself from the professional visitor category and move to complete the presentation.

Despite knowing this, many people are so worried about rejection that they are afraid to either ask for the order or attempt a closing. This lack of action creates a situation in which they must call back again. That peak of opportunity is often missed by the second meeting, because the prospect has cooled and an opportunity to be of service has been missed.

PEOPLE – will let you down, consciously or unconsciously. They are weak and fallible and are affected by fear, pride, anger, prejudice, frustration and ambition. Accepting this fact, and the fact that you too share some of those traits, will enable you to go forward with some degree of compassion, understanding and forgiveness. This will also enable you to be realistic in your expectations of and demands on others.

Only God will not let you down.

PERCEPTION – is usually affected by our perspective. Try to look at events and possibilities from the points of view or situations of others. This is good in business as well as life.

PERFORMANCE – Does your performance match the goals you have established?

PERSEVERANCE – Vince Lombardi, the legendary football coach, claimed that there wasn't a game his team could not have won, if the game had gone on long enough. He referred to stamina and determination as character in action. They are needed in order to stick to the tasks required for success, particularly in adverse conditions.

PERSISTENCE – is often more important than "smarts" when it comes to developing a business relationship (or any other type of relationship for that matter).

PERSONAL BUSINESS – If you start your day with personal business such as domestic chores, personal calls and dinner arrangements, you will probably find that day is substantially wasted in terms of business achievement. Try to schedule those tasks for the end of the day, after you have achieved something.

PERSONAL CONTACT – One of the most successful securities salesmen of the century was once described as: 1) preferring to go and see a person rather than telephoning; and 2) preferring not to deal with the prospect at all if he had to write a letter. Extreme or not, these forms of contact describe effectiveness in relation to proximity.

You are far more likely to get a positive response from a personal meeting, somewhat less likely from a telephone call and significantly less likely with a letter or mailing. Nothing cements relations like personal contact. Even if you have a monumental reputation, strive to meet your client, so that you have the understanding necessary to help him or her achieve his or her goals.

PERSONALITY TYPES – There are "can do," "can't do" and "won't do" people in all walks of life. Though they do not make a conscious decision to be in the latter two categories, most people are. Look at yourself honestly and decide to be in the first category – "can do" – then work at it each and every day.

Do not spend a great deal of time trying to work with "can't do" and "won't do" types.

PERSPECTIVE – It is very easy to lose your bearings during times of trial. Try to focus on what is important, good or right at these moments. Try to be grateful for something.

PETTINESS – Don't major in the minors. Get on with the bigger things.

PIPELINE – This is the inventory of prospects and qualified prospects you are developing as clients. Since it takes time to establish a business relationship, you must build and work on the pipeline or inventory of individuals you are contacting. Keep in mind, they are at different stages of becoming clients or users of your product.

PLANNING – After you have reviewed your daily performance (see Review), the next step is to plan the following day – to some extent. Arrange follow-up and service calls. Set up sales calls and add to the work of the previous day. Leave room for surprises and contingencies. Details should be noted in your phone log or desk diary.

You should have half the next day blocked out before leaving for the evening. This is not unreasonable. It's surprising how this step gets rid of many fears and usually has you looking forward to getting into the office the next day. It will also avert those "cold starts" that waste time in the morning.

POSSESSIONS – can possess us with their demands for time and attention. Travel light.

POOR CHOICES – Whether in business or in life, there is a cost to poor choices. Yet, we are always surprised when the bill comes due. These are conscious decisions we know are not right, but we continue to make them – for example, cutting corners, forgetting integrity and honesty, smoking, alcohol abuse, substance abuse, or simply over-eating. Just as in the old cowboy movies, there is always a cost for doing the wrong thing, but this time it's real.

POSITIVE/NEGATIVE RATIO – Always keep your positive comments, thoughts and ideas ahead of the negatives. Be known as a realistically positive, "can do" type of person, as opposed to being a negative faultfinder. Don't justify negatives on the basis of being realistic or helpful. "Accentuate the positive, eliminate the negative, latch on to the affirmative and don't mess with Mr. In-Between" – (40's song).

POSSIBILITIES – Try to see what is possible. It fires both energy and enthusiasm. As soon as you have grasped the possibilities, work at turning them into probabilities. It is that transition which leads to success.

PRESENTATIONS – Building blocks provide a model for sales presentations. The key reasons for action used in a presentation should build so that the prospect's only logical course of action is to proceed. (You should have no more than five or six points.) Each reason builds on the level established by the previous one. Visualize your presentation as a series of steps, leading to an inescapable conclusion. Clarity and simplicity are key. (See Peak.)

PRESSURE – Do not respond to pressure tactics. Try not to inflict pressure on others by using artificial time limits or the possibility of dire consequences. Lay out the facts truthfully. Do not try to force an issue with false threats of lost opportunity. Restating the key points with their inescapable conclusion is far more effective, even if the prospect has to "sleep on it."

The difference between enthusiasm and pressure is that one is attractive and the other self-promoting One fosters empathy, the other hostility.

PRIDE – is often used to cover feelings of insecurity or inadequacy. You can afford to be compassionate with prideful people. (See Humility.)

PRIORITIES – There should be a connection between business potential and time commitments. Take a moment to attempt to discern proper priorities before leaping into action.

PROBLEMS – Anybody can deal with one problem at a time. It's when you have four or five simultaneously that fear, despair and discouragement can set in. Remember, if one of them can't destroy you, the sum total can't bury you. Break them down into simple challenges and try to deal with each one separately, even if you have to assign specific times or days to deal with each one.

There is great relief as you conquer each one. Very often, attempting to help others with their problems helps to put yours into perspective. Don't rehearse problems with yourself or others. Put them into perspective by writing them down and then attempt to deal with them – if they should be dealt with. (See Adversity.)

PROCRASTINATION – most of us will use pride, fear, illness, fatigue, time of day, anger, resentment etc. – often negative emotions or thoughts – to help avoid doing the "do" things. The basis of procrastination is often fear of rejection. One of the best ways to overcome it is to become enthusiastic about something and try to get into action. Confidence and self esteem will follow. Careers, marriages and businesses often fail as a result of procrastination. (See Decisions.)

PRODUCT – Your product is an item or service which answers a need. You must understand how it works, why it works, and the underlying need it addresses. Matching the item or service with the need is selling. Occasionally, you must illustrate the need and elaborate on it to the prospective purchaser. Very often you are simply selling peace of mind.

Your product is the combination of yourself, your company, your associates, your skills and your ideas.

PROFANITY – Never, never use profanity or coarse language in a sales presentation. (It is a good idea to avoid it altogether.) You are a professional, and no matter what the prospect's manner of speech is, keep your standards high. Many salespeople remove themselves from serious consideration by trying to emphasize a point or describe a characteristic in an offensive manner. Also avoid using religious, ethnic or gender-sensitive terms in a tongue-in-cheek manner. This too, can be greatly offensive.

PROGRESS – Very often, progress is measured in inches. Do not be discouraged. As you look back, you will see the great distance you have travelled. Do not be upset by the seemingly greater progress of others. Your direction is what is important. You may catch them as they plateau or decline, or as you have spurts of growth, or possibly not at all. Your journey is what counts. Look up, instead of sideways.

PROMISES – Must be kept. Be careful and realistic when making them. If there is any uncontrollable change, let the other party know as soon as possible and seek a joint solution. A promise should really be made only when there cannot be unforeseen circumstances – therefore use them advisedly.

PROSPECT – This is a client or customer in waiting. For a variety of reasons, you have focused upon this individual as potentially requiring your product or services.

PROSPECTING – All selling careers begin with prospecting. The unfortunate fact is that many level off and end with little or no prospecting. If one were to draw a graph of many sales careers, it would show production moving up, then across and then down. The latter stages reflect the more fragile egos of older types, as well as fatigue, laziness, or just plain complacency with income levels. By combining these sensitivities with the fact that an existing client body is continually running down, it is easy to get the "loser curve" pattern of income.

This "loser curve" is typified by three phases:

1. Prospecting;
2. Servicing existing accounts only; and
3. The Run-Down phase, where existing accounts gradually disappear.

Huge producers never give up prospecting and when their business becomes too great, they add assistants. Many have become "companies" within their company, often with more real power and income than their C.E.Os.

PROSPECT SOURCES:

1. Family.
2. Friends.
3. Social Contacts (clubs, associations etc.).
4. Your suppliers (doctor, lawyer, accountant, dentist, butcher, plumber, gardener, landlord, pharmacist etc.).
5. Neighbours.
6. Lists from trade publications or directories.
7. Franchisees.
8. Publications – newspaper appointments, notices or profile articles which also give background.
9. Businesses – either in your area or indutrial park. Each is backed by at least one entrepreneur.

10. Past business associates.
11. Client referrals.
12. The product itself will often define possible prospects for you.

When you start to focus on what you do, what you have to offer, and the company you work for, potential customers will come to mind automatically. The problem will really become how to do something about all the names or raw prospects which come to mind. It will be like a flood.

PUNCTUALITY – Always arrive five minutes early for meetings. Remember, you are being judged, in part, before the meeting starts. Being late tells the prospect how unimportant the meeting or their business really is to you. It is also discourteous and irritating to someone who has scheduled time for you. Plan ahead. Consider weather, traffic and other contingencies. Use the cell phone if you are going to be unavoidably delayed.

PUT DOWNS – You cannot berate people into being successful. Negatives breed negatives. Do not accept put downs from others or from yourself. Build on people's assets rather than on their shortcomings.

Q

QUALIFIED PROSPECT – An individual who, after being contacted, has confirmed your original estimation of his or her need for your product or services. This appraisal should normally, but not always, be supported by some indication of further interest on his or her part.

QUALITY – means detail. It is the result of continually looking for small ways to be a little better, as well as ways to be a lot better. This is true for products, companies and individuals.

R

RANDOM WALK – Life is not a random walk – things rarely just happen. There are choices and consequences, causes and effects. Look at the things happening in your life and try to see your role in their occurrences. Looking at our actions and the results enables us to grow and benefit from what is going on around us. With awareness comes the responsibility for change. Seeking God's will in your life (as you understand it) is a good starting point for change.

Learn from others, both their good and bad choices.

REALITY – has a way of seeking you out. Address the real issues in life and business, not the substitutes.

R.E.D. – Rest, exercise and diet are important for success in the business marathon. Don't ignore any one of these.

REJECTION – is part of the cost of success. Achieving your goals is a function of the number of times you attempt to do business face-to-face. In trying to get those meetings, you will naturally have to deal with some rejection, occasionally even after a meeting. The better you handle rejection from prospects, the more clients you will end up having.

REFERRALS – A follow-up or service call is a logical opportunity to ask for a referral. Remember, your customer is on your side. It is up to you to show that person how both of you can help someone else.

The client's first-hand experience in dealing with you, through build-up, closing and follow-up, is now an asset. Many friends, associates and family members do not have, what you are providing for him or her. Your client's confidence in you and your product should be put to a profitable use for all concerned.

Don't wear out your welcome. Keep in mind that follow-up calls should not be used on every occasion to seek referrals.

RELATIONSHIPS – are good indicators of success. They are built on trust, respect and consideration. Money is important, in that it provides choices, but make sure your success is broadly based in the inter-personal sense. Work on your relationships, they pay real dividends.

RESENTMENT – is a killer and that is not an overstatement. Hanging on to old hurts can virtually destroy people and everything around them, as their lives become dominated by bitterness. Fear, anger and resentment are tied together by time. Fear is about the future – "I may not get what I want." Anger concerns the present – "I am not getting what I want." Resentment relates to the past – "I didn't get what I wanted." For this reason working on a faith in a loving God is important. As we get ourselves out of the centre of the universe God's plan can become more important to ours and the hurt diminishes. Pray for the people you resent, and it is amazing how this destructive feeling evaporates.

RESPECT – You cannot command it. You must earn it through your actions. It is a key ingredient in all relationships – business or otherwise. Have respect for yourself and for others.

RESOLUTIONS – Don't make New Year's resolutions. Make daily resolves. Great long-term (yes, a year is long-term) intentions really do not provide much in the way of guidance for action. The commitment to do something today does this. It is the build-up of positive and constructive daily actions which leads to long-term results.

RESPONSIBILITY – Each of us is responsible for our own actions and inaction. As soon as we stop blaming other people, places, or circumstances, we can get to work on ourselves and the things we wish to accomplish. When we have earned a prospect's trust, we have a responsibility to have his or her interests in mind. Neglecting those interests is the beginning of a downward slide.

RETIRE – Never retire. Always be involved, even if it is only a few days each week or as a volunteer. You have to be active and connected with people. Someone once said, "Don't retire, re-fire."

RETREAT – It is very hard to attack when you are retreating. Establish a point where you will stand, fight and renew the attack. Do not accept continuing setbacks as your lot in life. Often they happen because we allow them to or give them too great a priority in our thinking.

REVIEW – Take the time to compare your goals and your efforts to see if they match. Your work day should not be considered finished until you have re-examined your efforts and accomplishments. A few questions you might ask yourself are:

1. How did I allocate my time?
2. Did I focus on business potential?
3. Was I working smart?
4. Did I avoid closings? Why?
5. Were my presentations clear and enthusiastic?
6. What new accounts and/or prospects did I generate?
7. What needs to be followed up?
8. Did I do the "do things"?
9. What did I learn?

You may wish to build your own checklist and whatever form it takes – do it on a regular basis. Do your own time-and-motion study from your checklist. Are you functioning efficiently? Are you wasting time or throwing away days?

Do not make this review a totally negative exercise, and thus discourage yourself. Keep a positive focus on the things you are doing well, and the things you can improve on.

RISK – If you continually bet on 50:50 odds, it is a mathematical certainty that you will go bankrupt. Risks must be taken from time to time, but try to cut the odds against you. Ensure the rewards are commensurate with the risk you are taking.

RULES – are made for the many because of the few. Abide by them, don't bend them, ignore them or try to find a way around them. Be strict in your adherence to them.

S

SABOTAGE – as in self-sabotage. Don't worry about external enemies. Your main threat is riding around within you. Many people, particularly talented ones, are so afraid of failing that they never really try. Somehow, they rationalize that this is not really failure. They would rather have the fantasy of success than the possible reality of mediocrity, or direction toward another area. Let your ideas stand the test of reality – try them. You may stumble, but eventually you will succeed. It is those who try, who succeed.

SALES – The effective communication of an idea or concept in order to influence actions and events.

SALEVICE – This should be a real word because sales and service are so interconnected and, in practice, inseparable.

SAME SIDE – Be on the same side as your prospect or client in an effort to address his or her goals. The prospect is not an adversary. Your job is to identify and empathize with them. When the client feels that you are working toward a solution in his or her best interests, you have the beginning of a long-term and mutually beneficial relationship. Prospects know when your interests are being put ahead of their own.

SAVINGS – Make a habit of regularly putting some funds aside. Having some money available will help you to think and function more effectively, and concentrate on your clients' needs, versus your own.

SAY – what you do and do what you say. This is a key ingredient for success.

SELF-IMAGE – A positive self-image results from, and is affected by, the things we do or don't do. In this regard, responsible or considerate actions, which may not even lead to profit or gain, help us as much as anything or anyone. Work at developing a positive self-image. If you see yourself as a failure or as someone who will never succeed, you will tend to accept negatives as reality and as pertaining to you. If you envision yourself as successful, the negatives will be seen simply as irritants or material for your autobiography. A positive self-image is a key ingredient to expecting and demanding success and to overcoming adversity. Do not hang onto things that undermine your self-image such as bad habits, beat-up cars or worn out clothes.

SELF-JUSTIFICATION – shuts off constructive inputs.

SEMINARS – Sales presentations with more than a few people present. Do not give out written material until after you have said what you want to say – unless, of course, you like your prospects reading while you're talking. When giving a monologue, you can count on no more than ten minutes of attention. You can extend this time frame if you are up and moving around. Use a board (not simply overhead slides) which you can mark up to show points graphically. People relate to graphic presentations and body language. The combined effect of additional stimuli will keep the crowd more alert and open to what you are saying. Stick to a basic, common-sense, building block presentation.

SERVICE – is the key to corporate survival and growth. Service is providing that unexpected "extra" or going that extra mile. Service is not a word, it is an action or a series of actions. Most clients are lost due to lack of service or consideration.

SETBACKS – make us stronger. They force us to review, learn, change, grow and overcome. All major successes appear to come out of setbacks and difficulties. They give birth to the determination to persevere. Any fool can benefit from success, but great men are blessed through their setbacks. What is the positive message or teaching you can gain from your setback?

SHAME – You can't shame people into success. Negatives breed negatives.

SHORTCOMINGS – Get going with what you have and who you are. Try to improve as you move forward. Don't spend too much time fretting about your shortcomings or negatives. Leave that for others, should they wish to do so.

SHOW UP – Former President George Bush once claimed that success is often based on simply showing up. You don't have to run yourself ragged going to everything, but find reasons to show up rather than not. You'll be surprised how opportunities then pop up. (See Availability.)

SILENCE – is an important part of selling. It allows your client or prospect to assist you with the information you need in order to be of service. Don't interrupt, it can shut off inputs or sidetrack a key point. You know what you know, find out what your client or prospect knows or believes.

SIMPLICITY – Keep it simple. In presentations ask yourself: "What are the key factors?" Remember, you have a very short time to present your case effectively. Excessively complex presentations rarely succeed. Simplicity usually gets results. Keep both your presentations and thought processes simple. (See Common Sense.)

SIZE – Don't worry too much about big competitors. People deal with people. It is not the size of the dog in the fight, it is the size of the fight in the dog that is important.

SKILLS – Prior to joining your company, you had the basic skills needed to start (degrees, courses, practical knowledge etc.). Part of your job is to build, refine, update and focus those skills in order to benefit your prospects and clients.

You can achieve this by reading any and all publications specific to your business on a regular basis. This includes periodicals, research reports, news services, background books and general newspapers. Specific product material should be read and re-read so that your knowledge is thorough and reflexive. This will greatly add to your confidence during presentations.

Know everything that you can about your competitors, so you can explain why your product is the best.

Ask about your firm's ideas, views, strategies and offerings. There are no foolish questions. The only foolish thing is not being informed. Before or after hours is the best time to seek information or clarify ideas.

SOURCES – Use newspapers, associations, clubs, family, friends, enemies, competitors, suppliers, people selling to you, everyone and everything. Be sensitive to relationships or this exercise can become negative. Don't be afraid, however, to ask your clients and friends if they know of anyone who would benefit from your contacting them. People don't like to be used, but if you are legitimately trying to be of service and address the needs of others, they appreciate that fact.

In your conversations, casually include your ideas, views and what you are doing. They soften the terrain for later contact. Remember, however, not to dominate all conversations with your business. Yet, don't be so anonymous that no one knows what you do. People like dealing with their friends, so use opportunities to convert social connections into business connections.

Always be selling, so have your cards and business material with you at all times. When you are shopping on a Saturday or chatting with a repairman, be prepared to present your card. Be ready to convert a contact into a mutually beneficial relationship.

Keep focused on clients and prospects and use what you have to assist them, even if no direct business will result. People are always grateful for that little extra effort or input, or just for having a person think of their needs. This will separate you from the pack.

SPEAK – positively about customers and associates. In fact, we should probably add everyone to this list. Looking for the best in people and speaking positively about them, programs our thinking in terms of gratitude and illustrates a respect for others. This does not mean that when something or someone is wrong we ignore it. It is usually better to speak to the party involved, rather than about them.

SPIRITUAL – The spiritual basis of a person's life is like the operating system of a computer. It is the "how" and "why" an individual conducts his or her life. It is also a point of reference or compass bearing in adversity. It gives the assurance of victory. Instead of bobbing like a cork from peak to trough, we are able to cut through adversity and grow. Spiritual vacuums do not exist. If you do not have a good operating basis, you have a flawed one.

STATUS – In the great quest for fame and fortune aim for fortune and see if that doesn't cover most of what you want. There is no upside to fame. For example, many individuals feel that they are "only" salespeople. Keep in mind that nothing happens until someone sells something to someone else. This is the central fact supporting all free enterprise economies and the advanced standards of living they generate. By addressing the needs of others, an honest and professional salesperson has the opportunity to earn whatever he or she may wish. They have an open invitation to contact anyone who can benefit from their products.

Don't worry about titles. Be of real service to your clients and prospects, and the president will be asking you to lunch.

STRENGTH – comes from doing. You get better as you go. Strength and energy come from action, not the other way around. You haven't used all your strength until you have asked God to help you. His power is essential for His work.

STUBBORN – Being stubborn can be good, if you are right. The problem is that most of us are not right all of the time. Ask yourself: "How important is it?" or "What is the real cost of being stubborn on an issue?" Ask others for input as to the merits of your stance. Success often comes more from correcting mistakes quickly and limiting their damage, than from being stubborn. Stubbornness and insecurity often go together and are negatives.

SUBSTANCE – is on the inside. It is what multiplies. The acorn is an example. One might see it simply as it is, or as a tree, or even a forest. Aim at building substance in yourself and try to recognize it in others.

SUBSTITUTES – Avoid substitutes for accomplishment and/or real effort. Many people avoid the steps or actions necessary for success because of fear or fatigue. Some accept second or third-best alternatives in lieu of results or goals.

SUCCESS – is the result of combining abilities with discipline. The bonding agent is the desire to succeed. This provides the motivation to grow in knowledge and skill, that is, to persevere in the things one must do for success. Too often, truly talented people fall by the wayside because of the inability or unwillingness to progress by working hard. Assume success, see yourself as successful and then act accordingly. (See Self-Image.) Business success has two aspects: first, letting people know that you can do a thing well, and second, doing it well.

SUPPORTING MATERIAL – should be prepared and available for meetings. Do not give it to the prospect until after your presentation, unless you want him or her to read while you are talking.

SURPASS – Go beyond what you have done before. Keep escalating your goals as you achieve them. Keep climbing.

T

TARGET – Aim for larger prospects and work on developing a relationship over time. Eventually, with intelligent persistence, they will become clients. Have a full pipeline of potential major accounts, as well as daily prospects.

TEACHABLE – Stay teachable. Do not shut off inputs because of pride or fear. The learning process in business and life never ends.

TEAM – Teams can accomplish much more than individuals. Function as a team member – passing the ball, giving credit and keeping other members informed.

TELEPHONE LOG – Keep a telephone log of the calls you have set up for each day. One good plan is to have your topics listed across the top of the page and your prospects down the left side. Use a form of shorthand in the resulting boxes, such as an "o" for what you wish to talk about, a check mark for an order, an "X" for no order, "CII" for they will call if interested or "CA" for you'll call again and "CB" for they will call back. Post unfinished business on the next day's sheet.

At the end of the day, if there are few marks in your telephone log, then you'll know the problem is you. Staying organized in this way will give you a clear analysis of your efforts and results.

Set up tomorrow's calls today, leaving some room for contingencies.

TENACITY – Sticking to a goal, especially in adversity, is what success demands and legends are made of.

It usually takes a minimum of five contacts to move a prospect into the client category. Not sticking to this routine will actually wear you down after a period of time. Eventually you will slacken off prospecting altogether. An old prospector friend of mine once told me about not paddling his canoe around a point of land because he was fed up.

He later heard that around the point, a massive gold-bearing quartz vein extended right into the lake, such that anyone passing could not miss it. It became a major gold mine. Go the distance.

Many prospects are the recipients of "one shot" or "fly by" sale efforts which they find both time consuming and self-serving. This is usually the reason for a cold or hostile initial contact response. As you make a continuing effort to be of service, you will separate yourself from the pack.

THANK – people and God for all things, large and small. Everyone appreciates being appreciated.

TIMING – It is natural for keen and aggressive salespeople to start their cold calls first thing in the morning. This is often a busy time for prospects. Many successful salespeople do their prospecting late in the day. Most presidents and senior corporate officers are still in the office after five o'clock and usually after six. This is the time when they can take a few minutes to discuss a new product, concept or personal requirement.

Blocking out a certain time each day to make prospecting or sales calls has a great deal of merit. It enables you to get ready and helps to avoid the tendency to procrastinate.

TIME DRAINS – The following list of time drains is certainly not all-inclusive, but you might find some old friends here:

1. Spending time with substitutes for productive activity.
2. Not planning a task or thinking it through.
3. Too much office socializing.
4. Accepting interruptions and distractions.
5. Concentrating on micro issues.
6. Putting personal matters ahead of business.

TIME LIMITS – Stick to the time requested for the meeting. If you have asked for fifteen minutes, then respect what you have been given, unless the client specifically asks you to stay longer. This is part of that dependability discussed earlier. If you stay within your self-imposed and stated limits, the door will usually be open in the future. If you do not, it probably will not be.

Meet deadlines for commitments or projects. Often you are part of a unit that must fit together on time. Advise of problems early.

TOYS – do not add to our sense of self worth. They are fun to have, but our accomplishments are what build us.

TRANSITION – Something new from something old. We often miss what is going on until after it has happened. Usually, all we sense at the time is difficulty or pain. Moving forward can be hard and frightening. As we look back, we can often see God's hand in our lives through changes in direction. The in – between times are sometimes hard, but they do not last.

TRUST – J. P. Morgan once said that if you couldn't trust a man, you shouldn't be dealing with him. Remember this when dealing with others, and work on being trustworthy yourself.

TRUTH – Those who aren't ready for the truth are usually ready to argue. Always deal in the truth. People don't need to know every detail of a transaction, but they do need to know and understand the salient or important points. Don't bend the truth or skirt around it.

TOUGHNESS – is not measured by what you can do to others, but by what you yourself can endure.

U

UNDERESTIMATED – Being underestimated can be a great advantage. The pressure to succeed comes only from you and the opposition is off guard. Who would have thought in the 40s or 50s that Harry Truman would be remembered as one of the great American presidents? Helmut Kohl, the person most responsible for German reunification, claimed that being continually underestimated was one of his greatest advantages.

V

VALUE – Offer value in your products, service and relationships. Look at the other person's side, and ask if you would enter into this transaction or relationship. Do not be stingy of spirit in your dealings.

W

WASTE – If you are paying attention, very little is ever wasted. Time or money lost can often be profitable, if you learn the lesson of trying to get the best out of everything that happens in your life.

WINNERS – are not whiners.

WORDS – are important. They express thoughts, concepts and images. They have meaning. They convey ideas greater than their sum total, and occasionally different from one's intent. Don't throw them around carelessly. Strive for meaningful communication. Be clear.

WORK SMART – Develop discernment when it comes to the productive use of your time. Allocate time in relation to potential. Know what is important and what is not. Hard work is not a substitute for smart work. Always be looking for a better way.

Work when you work and play when you play. Block out time to do both, but don't kid yourself by trying to do both at the same time. Work can be fun, but focus on the task to be done. Work in short bursts and then take time to relax.

Remember that failures use up more energy being failures than successes use being successes.

WRITE – Keep a notebook and mark off your tasks and commitments as they are completed. You can feel your progress, even on a slow day. (See Organization.)

Write down prospects' names or ideas as they occur to you.

This task should include the use of a notebook (with you all the time), a desk diary to plan the future, and a telephone log to block out each day and provide a basis for your daily reviews.

You may wish to use your computer or organizer, but many find writing to be easier, faster and in meetings, quieter.

WRONG – It is not wrong to be wrong, but it is wrong to stay wrong. If something is not working – fix it or change it. Be open to other possibilities.

Y

YOU – can achieve what you want to as long as you are prepared to pay the price. By focusing all your efforts and energy on a particular goal, you can achieve anything. Be sure it is worth it.

YOURSELF – know yourself, like yourself, then forget yourself. Get on with life and focus on addressing the needs of others. You will then be taken care of. It is a matter of both faith and fact. (See Focus.)

Z

ZEAL – That enthusiastic sense of conviction or belief in what you are doing or trying to accomplish is a key ingredient for success. It must, however, be tempered with skill and understanding. (See Enthusiasm.)

ZZZ – Get enough rest and sleep. Fatigue and fear go together. Vince Lombardi once said, "fatigue makes cowards of us all." Be up for any task by being well rested. The same is true for getting enough exercise and proper nutrition.